Preface

Like many people, I often fluctuated between being a saver and a spender. When I entered the workforce in my early 20's, I was definitely more of the latter. I quickly learned that this was not sustainable and a waste of all the hard work I was putting in. I wondered why most of my money was going towards interest payments and paying off credit cards instead of bolstering my own finances.

I, therefore, decided to learn how to manage my money better and since then I can honestly say I have never looked back. These are a few of the lessons I learned throughout my career which I thought I would share with anyone who, like me, wishes to get out of debt and stay on the path towards financial freedom and security.

Table of Contents

1. Mindset
2. Debt
3. Compounding
4. Goal Setting
5. Self-Discipline
6. Inflation
7. Diversification
8. Education
9. Taking Control
10. Shop Around
11. Conclusion

1. Mindset

Creating true wealth,

Will often start slow.

The first step is determining,

Where your money goes.

Tracking your spending,
Must always come first.
For you can only invest,
What is in your purse.

Living with debt,

Is like drowning at sea.

So learning to save,

Should be your priority.

Maximise your ability,

To save and invest.

Once you achieve this,

Your goals can be met.

2. Debt

Debt is a tool,

That can sometimes be used,

So make sure you know how,

Before it decides to use you.

Only take loans,

For the things you will buy,

That will steadily increase,

In value over time.

If you're having difficulty,

Managing so many debts,

Try consolidating them into one,

So that your distraction is less.

When you take out a card,

With a high spending limit.

Ask your bank to reduce it,

So that you are comfortable with it.

Give yourself room,

If you take out a loan,

To ensure that your payments,

Are sustainable long term.

Having the funds,

To write off a debt,

Means you can sleep soundly,

At night in your bed.

3. Compounding

The beauty of compounding,

Is that there's nothing to do,

Except watch it grows faster,

On interest that's accrued.

Compound interest,

Time and again,

Has proven itself,

To be your best friend.

Small monthly payments,

May not seem like much.

But trust me, you'll notice,

When the numbers add up.

Every pound you invest,

Every dollar you save,

Will build up your wealth,

And make for a much brighter day.

Interest accrues,

At an extraordinary rate.

The longer you leave it,

The more it will make.

4. Goal Setting

Having a goal,

That's set in your mind,

Will give you the willpower,

To save over time.

Break down your goals,

Into very small steps,

So you're not overwhelmed,

And your aims can be met.

Take small amounts,

And tuck them away,

As they build up over time,

You'll find a nest egg awaits.

Once you have set,

A goal in your mind,

It's much easier to show patience,

Until the right time.

5. Self-Discipline

Before you decide,

To spend all your cash,

Ask yourself honestly,

"Do I really need that?"

Resisting the urge,

To buy frivolous things,

Will mean what you buy,

Will have greater meaning.

Like a hammer or a saw,

Money is a tool.

So look after it well,

So that it can look after you.

As most things depreciate,
Over long periods of time,
Try to buy assets,
Whose value will rise.

6. Inflation

Remember the value,

Of money decreases.

So investing in assets,

Is the smart way to defeat this.

Year upon year,

You'll see prices will rise.

So as much as you can be,

With your money, be wise.

That dollar or pound,

Which you worked so hard to earn,

Won't buy the same things,

A year or two down the road.

Prices will rise,

Of that you can be assured,

So sometimes fixed rates,

Can be the option most secure.

7. Diversification

Spreading your savings,

And investments around,

Will bring you much lower risk,

Should an investment go down.

Generating passive income,
Is the key to ensure,
That your money is working,
As hard as you are.

Income that's passive,

Is smart and is wise.

It works while you sleep,

So it's buying you time.

Start a new business,

And try, try again.

For it is only persistence,

That wins in the end.

8. Education

Knowledge is wealth,

So learn all that you can.

So your decisions are based,

Not on rumours but facts.

Seek out advice,

From reputable sources.

For the more you discover,

Will bolster your choices.

Learn well from others,

The good and the bad.

So that you're already ahead,

When you draw up your plan.

Making mistakes,

Is never a sin.

But don't keep on repeating,

Again and again.

9. Taking Control

Keep track of your spending,

And try to ensure,

That the income you bring,

Is at least equal or more.

Check your deductions,

On your paycheck from work,

So that the remainder that's yours,

Can be put hard to work.

Keeping good records,

Of the money you make,

Means it's easier to see,

Where savings can be made.

10. Shop Around

Keep up to date,

With the best deals around,

And move your money accordingly,

Not lying around.

Comparison sites,

Are wonderful tools,

For getting great deals,

From insurance to fuel.

11. Conclusion

"Save often and regularly,

Spend only when needed,"

Is the sagest advice,

Which will benefit when heeded.